No Computer Viruses

By J Lynn

ISBN-13: 978-1466274075
ISBN-10: 1466274077

First Computer

In 1984, I bought my first home computer system from Radio Shack. At that time, I had to finance the computer, monitor, dot matrix printer, extra floppy drive, and extra memory. A hard drive was not available then. The total cost of all the equipment (computer system) was $2,300.00, not including interest charges. In 2009 the equivalent computer system could be purchased from around $600 to $800.00 (this is constantly changing) depending on where you purchase the equipment.

In 1984, the computer processor speed was 2.1 MHz. In 2009 a common computer speed could be 2,600 MHz or 2.6 Gig Hz. This is a thousand times faster than the one purchased in 1984. The cost of purchasing new personal computers has evolved, not unlike that of buying a common commodity like a toaster.

I started using Microsoft disk operating systems(DOS), 2.1, and continued using them up to Windows XP64. I stopped using Microsoft operating systems software, after this Windows version, unless I am paid to do so (such as at work). I had experienced all the flaws, disappointments, viruses, spyware, malware, and the blue screens of death that came with using this operating systems software. I found myself spending more time trying to keep this software updated and fixed than using it. I reached the point where I wanted a better operating system, one that didn't take up so much of my free time just to keep it working.

Microsoft Requires Faster Processing Speeds

Home computers today have to be faster in order to work with the new Microsoft 7 operating systems software. Each time Microsoft introduces a new operating system software, it requires more processing power hardware and memory to operate. The software is becoming a memory hog with all the required processes that are operating in the background. You will not be able to install Windows 7 on an older computer because it will not boot up and run due to the lack of hardware capabilities. Dedicated Microsoft users have become used to these hardware requirements for each newer software revision release. For them it is how progression works.

Software Bit Size RISC

RISC (reduced instruction set computing) was used to make software run faster.

This has to do with the way operating software processes the size of data bit per cycle. The oldest software processed eight bits at a cycle. In 2010 common operating systems software for the home computer processes up to 64 bits per computer cycle. Older software actually runs faster on computers because it requires less processing power, memory, and time to finish an instruction set. Older operating system software still in use today such as 16 bit Linux software will process faster than that of 32 or 64 bit Microsoft operating system software on the same RISC computer.

Older computers that were designed for 16 bit operating systems are too slow to run on 32 or 64 bit Microsoft software. People have been lead to believe that their computer systems are too old and slow to work with the newer Microsoft operating system software that is developed every two or three years. However, these computers will work fine with other non-windows operating system software. These people will discard or throw away their old systems to get the newest and greatest operating system already installed when they purchase a new computer. Because the newer Microsoft software will not work on the older computers. Microsoft has designed this by default with the newer software becoming processing and memory hogs. Requiring people to buy newer computer systems, with the latest software programs containing all the bells and whistles.

Moore's Law

Each time the bit size of the operating system software is increased, the more processing power, memory size, and speed is required to keep the system from running very slowly, or will not work at all. This is what Microsoft tries to make their dedicated users believe. The computer hardware tends to follow Moore's Law of doubling in processing power every 18 months. However, the software takes years to try and catch up with the hardware. Microsoft is one popular software that has tried to come out with a new operating system every three years, even if the software is not completely bug free (Microsoft forces their programs into the market, knowing they are not problem-free, in order to get their product to the market first, and to fix them at a later date).

Misleading Advertisements

One of the most disturbing commercials on the radio, TV, and the Internet is for the need to buy products for all computers to keep them running faster and to prevent them from getting infected with viruses, spy ware, registry errors and computer crashes (computers will display some kind of message, or freeze up, or keeps rebooting). These advertisements are mostly for the Windows computer systems, and not for other operating systems, such as Macs, or Linux. Most of these problems exist only for the Windows operating software systems. A whole new industry has been created around the Microsoft Windows operating systems flaws. Here are some web site examples to help you fix your troubled Windows computers: www.doublemyspeed.com, www.cleanmypc.com, www.maxmyspeed.com and www.fixmypc.com that are for profit only software companies. These companies only exist for Windows computer users.

Some Truth in Advertisements

One of the advertisements that is running today has some truth in it, that you don't have to buy a new computer to have a faster running pc. You don't even have to buy new expensive software to make your computer run faster and have all the bells and whistles. There are other software operating systems that will do this but in general Microsoft users are reluctant to try some other operating systems software such as Linux even if it free to obtain. Most Microsoft users are reluctant to switch even when they know how flawed their software is.

Computer Software Viruses and Malware

It has been stated that as many as 40,000 new viruses have been already created with new viruses written each and everyday for Microsoft Windows software. In the last 10 years, less than 50 viruses have been written for Linux operating systems software. Windows users constantly use their anti-virus checkers to monitor for a virus infection. The Windows security world is about protection-for-profit software firms and these firms are the first to find and offer protection against viruses, spy-ware or malware.

These software protection-for-profit programs are really infective because they find a fix after virus has infected a number of computers and these people need help. This brings back memories of the I Love You virus that was a computer worm that successfully attacked tens of millions of computers in 2000 when it was sent as an attachment to a user with the text "ILOVEYOU" in the subject line. I have a friend that used only Windows operating system that was infected with the Conficker. This virus was a computer worm that targeting the Microsoft Windows operating system that was first detected in November 2008. My friend requested my help since there was no anti-virus program that could fix his computer at that time. We used a computer program to wipe his hard disk as a last resort and tried to re-install Windows again. He was not able to re-install Windows because of virus. I suggested that he try installing Linux Ubuntu. I was using this Linux at that time and was familiar with it. This Linux program installed without any problems and the virus that could not be removed had no effect. This fix saved my friend from throwing away his hard drive and buying a new one. My friend is still using this hard today years later and is now a Linux user that will only use Windows on a different computer for an older proprietory software program for his business. Everything else is used on his Linux Ubuntu computer. He is a believer after all his different grown up children and friends have since became infected on their Windows computers. He has converted them to Linux.

If you are unlucky enough to have a rogue program find a weakness or opening in your Windows software, you could end up paying up to $200 per infection to have your machine sanitized by a local computer repair shop. This security flaw helps firms to sell protection for profit software and to reinforce the need to have malware protection. These malware firms are aware of this Windows software weakness and base all of their advertising on the insecure fears of Windows users. This is where the conditions become right for these firms to peddle their fixes. These firms have conditioned Windows users to accept these fixes as the norm.

Windows users look at me in disbelief when I tell them that these flaws are mostly a Windows problem that does not apply to Linux users. Windows users have come to expect to pay for their false sense of security that these software firms sell them. I have tried to explain to many of the Windows users that the permissions on Linux software make the need for these security software programs unnecessary. One of the things that I have explained to Windows users is that when you download from the Internet using Fire Fox web browser you only have user installation permission by default. This makes installing viruses or malware difficult to do on Linux OS. These permissions cover three things that you can do with files on your Linux computer they are read, write, and execute. The permissions only allow you to install on Linux in three levels. One for the root (administrator) user, for the individual user that has is signed in, and for all others. By default, any software program that can change the system requires root (Administrator) permissions to run or to be installed.

Microsoft operating system software by design (default) grants administrative permissions to any one or intruders the ability to execute software on your computer system. Microsoft justifies this security flaw by saying it adds to the user experience of the Web site if this site can do remarkable things on your desktop. This flaw gives access for those firms that make money by providing additional security or fixing the harm that has been caused to your computer software from viruses or malware. Malware authors know that their infections will in all likelihood be executed and will do the malware instructions without ever asking for permissions on a Windows computer. Sometimes malware programs will require that an attachment be open while others will not. By what ever means, malware on Windows computer will often get executed and infect the computer. Once it completes its infection, the malware will then start spreading the infection to other Window computer systems. A virus can even forward some infections through your Microsoft office email to your mailing lists disguising the forwards as if you had sent the mail.

Why is Linux safer

One of the more interesting observations of Linux is the diversity of the Linux distributions. This way of deployment is one reason why Linux is safer than Windows. a case in point, a malicious .deb distribution would only work on Debian, Ubuntu, Mint, Mepis, or other Debian system. A RPM, YUM, Portage, Entropy, Pacman, slackpkg, and etc. systems would be exempt from an infection. Tarballs which are a type of Zipped file are all together another type way to download a distribution system.

A huge safeguard built into Linux distribution system is the mammoth size of the repositories of the most popular distributions. These resources help keep users safer because they won't need to use a search engine to download from untrusted sources.

On Linux operating systems, computers have a built-in protection against malware infected files from your email client or Web browser. If malware infections try renaming your files to something else that will not help. Because Linux and its applications don't depend on file extension names to identify the properties of a file. Linux prevents the user from mistakenly executing a malware program with these default permissions.

New users that move to Linux OS are freed from having to purchase a security software program to protect themselves from malware. However, Linux is not virus or malware proof. Linux users must be aware of viruses the same as users of other operating systems have to be alert of security issues, and take precautions to keep their systems safe and secure. Users should never run programs with root (administrative) privileges when it is not required, and they should install new update security fixes as they become available. You simply don't need anti-virus products to keep your Linux computer free of malware. No matter what deceptive claims, and false advertisers of virus protection for-profit companies say.

Linux users are infinitely more security conscious and have free access to lots of intrusion and vulnerability testing software. The amount of people that test the software out number Microsoft testers in the millions around the world who do this without even being paid.

An old adage that has been said is that a system is only as secure as the users' ability to secure it sums most of the feelings of safety in the Linux community. Even though Linux is inherently more secure by design, users need to be relentless in keeping their systems safe.

On April 10, 2008 the he number of computer viruses that were circulating the Internet reached one million. The majority of these infections had infected Windows computer that were connected to the Internet. Since 2003, Mac computers were no longer immune to viruses and the rate of infections have been increasing each year. The bottom line with Apple users is that they still feel more comfortable using an Apple than a (Windows) PC. Apple's OS X system was designed to be Internet safe right out of the box. They felt this system could be used on the Internet without the need for firewalls or any additional security software.

Chocolate And Linux

Chocolate and Linux operating systems have have one thing in common. They come in a multitude of different flavors and types. Another thing that people can agree on is that not every one likes the same flavor whether it is Chocolate or a Linux operating system. I have found that you have to try different flavors to find the one you like best. Most are good but the individual's flavor will be determined by that person. I can make a recommendation but each person have different tastes. Operating systems are constantly changing and a person's taste can change. I have changed which operating systems I like best over time. This change over time is what keeps it interesting with new innovations introduced constantly updated.

Microsoft Windows' Blue Screen of Death

The Blue Screen of Death is one of the most dreaded software errors or flaws in the Windows world. Jokingly called the blue screen of death because when the error occurs, the screen turns blue, and the computer almost always freezes and requires rebooting. The famous Blue Screen of Death (BSOD) will pop up on a Windows operating system whenever something has gone intolerably wrong. Here are a couple of examples of the many BSOD that can occur with the different Microsoft Windows operating systems software:

```
A problem has been detected and windows has been shut down to prevent damage
to your computer.

DRIVER_IRQL_NOT_LESS_OR_EQUAL

if this is the first time you've seen this stop error screen,
restart your computer. If this screen appears again, follow
these steps:

Check to make sure any new hardware or software is properly installed.
If this is a new installation, ask your hardware or software manufacturer
for any windows updates you might need.

if problems continue, disable or remove any newly installed hardware
or software. Disable BIOS memory options such as caching or shadowing.
If you need to use Safe Mode to remove or disable components, restart
your computer, press F8 to select Advanced startup options, and then
select Safe Mode.

Technical information:

*** STOP: 0x000000D1 (0x00000000, 0x00000002, 0x00000000, 0xFCBAC2A4)

***    CRASHDD.SYS - Address FCBAC2A4 base at FCBAC000, Datestamp 36bb6f3c

Beginning dump of physical memory
Dumping physical memory to disk: 100
Physical memory dump complete.
Contact your system administrator or technical support group for further
assistance.
```

```
*** STOP: 0x0000000A (0x802aa502,0x00000002,0x00000000,0xFA84001C)
IRQL_NOT_LESS_OR_EQUAL*** Address fa84001c has base at fa840000 - i8042prt.SYS

CPUID: GenuineIntel 5.2.c irql:1f    SYSVER 0xF0000565

Dll Base  Date Stamp  - Name                 Dll Base  Date Stamp  - Name
80100000  2be154c9   - ntoskrnl.exe          80400000  2bc153b0   - hal.dll
80200000  2bd49628   - ncrc710.sys           8025c000  2bd49688   - SCSIPORT.SYS
80267000  2bd49683   - scsidisk.sys          802a6000  2bd496b9   - Fastfat.sys
fa800000  2bd49666   - Floppy.SYS            fa810000  2bd496db   - Mpfs_Rec.SYS
fa820000  2bd49676   - Null.SYS              fa830000  2bd4965a   - Beep.SYS
fa840000  2bdaab00   - i8042prt.SYS          fa850000  2bd5a020   - SERMOUSE.SYS
fa860000  2bd4966f   - kbdclass.SYS          fa870000  2bd49671   - MOUCLASS.SYS
fa880000  2bd9c0be   - Videoprt.SYS          fa890000  2bd49638   - NCR77C22.SYS
fa0a0000  2bd4a4ce     Vga.SYS               fa0b0000  2bd496d0     Msfs.SYS
fa8c0000  2bd496c3   - Npfs.SYS              fa8e0000  2bd496c9   - Ntfs.SYS
fa940000  2bd496df   - NDIS.SYS              fa930000  2bd49707   - wdlan.sys
fa970000  2bd49712   - TDI.SYS               fa950000  2bd5a7fb   - nbf.sys
fa980000  2bd72406   - streams.sys           fa9b0000  2bd4975f   - ubnb.sys
fa9c0000  2bd5bfd7   - mcsxus.sys            fa9d0000  2bd4971d   - netbios.sys
fa9e0000  2bd49678   - Parallel.sys          fa9f0000  2bd4969f   - serial.SYS
faa00000  2bd49739   - mup.sys               faa40000  2bd4971f   - SMBTRSUP.SYS
faa10000  2bd6f2a2   - srv.sys               faa50000  2bd4971a   - afd.sys
faa60000  2bd6fd80   - rdr.sys               faaa0000  2bd49735   - bowser.sys

Address  dword dump  Build [1381]                       - Name
fe9cdaec fa84003c fa84003c 00000000 00000000 80149905   - i8042prt.SYS
fe9cdaf8 8025dfe0 8025dfe0 ff8e6b8c 80129c2c ff8e6b94   - SCSIPORT.SYS
fe9cdb10 8013e53a 8013e53a ff8e6b94 00000000 ff8e6b94   - ntoskrnl.exe
fe9cdb18 8010a373 8010a373 ff8e6df4 ff8e6f60 ff8e6c58   - ntoskrnl.exe
fe9cdb38 80105683 80105683 ff8e6f60 ff8e6c3c 8015ac7e   - ntoskrnl.exe
fe9cdb44 80104722 80104722 ff8e6df4 ff8e6f60 ff8e6c58   - ntoskrnl.exe
fe9cdb4c 8012034c 8012034c 00000000 80088000 80106fc0   - ntoskrnl.exe

Restart and set the recovery options in the system control panel
or the /CRASHDEBUG system start option. If this message reappears,
contact your system administrator or technical support group.
```

Install Linux operating software and Kiss the Blue Screen of Death goodbye!

Is Your PC Too Old?

Is your computer too old to work with the new Windows operating system software such as Windows 7 but still works with Windows 98, Windows 2000, and Windows XP? Do you want to keep and use your old pc just for the Internet and word processing but don't want to spend hundreds of dollars to keep it up to date with current software?

Different Linux operating software is available for old computers to the present processing speeds that will make the computer run as fast as the newest home computers. Removal of the old operating system such as Microsoft and installing the right Linux operating system will make the computer work fast like it did when it was first purchased. The right Linux software needed to install will depend on the memory and the processor speed. One of the slower computer processor (older computers) that can be made to run faster with success is recommended to start from a 400 MHz processor with at least 120 megabyte of memory. This is the minimum speed that works well with all the older Linux software that you will generally need and still be able to access the Internet. Puppy Linux version 4.1.2.1 works well with these older computers. This software can be downloaded from **www.distrowatch.com** or from Puppy's website:

Here is Puppy's website screen shot:

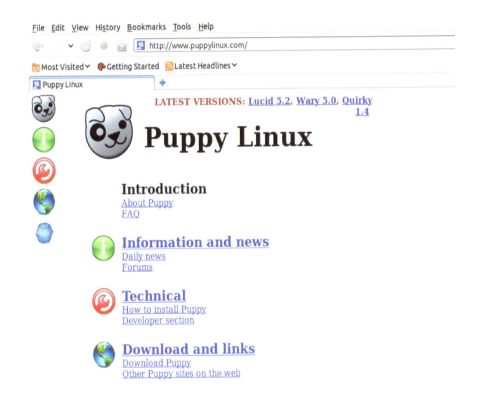

Using a high speed Internet connection such as DSL or faster and Linux software will make your older computer seem to run as fast as a brand new computer.

A processor with 800 MHz speed will run the newer software that has more advanced features and updates. Different versions of Linux operating systems and add-on software are available free over the Internet for download with a high speed DSL or satellite connection. Many different flavors of Linux are available from one web site such as **www.distrowatch.com**. This web site offers Linux operating software systems from the newest and most preferred. Also this website has older versions of software available for free. Distrowatch also offers the operating systems available on a live (try it before you install it) install CD for just the cost of the CD and shipping charge. The web site has software such as Ubuntu Linux 10.10 for $1.95 on a CD and a 4GB USB flash drive with the software for about $21.95 (prices change without notice). Also this website has the newest Linux software and beta versions for trial.

Here is an example of the **www.distrowatch.com** web page:

Ubuntu has been rated as the number one Linux downloaded software for some time. The over all ease of the install and use process has made it the number one download available for Linux users or newcomers. This version has metamorphosed to one of the easiest to use by beginners. Ubuntu can be downloaded from **www.ubuntu.com**.

Here is a screen shot of their web page.

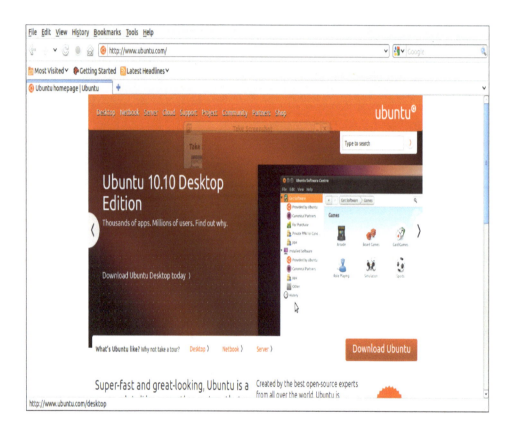

Installing Ubuntu From A Live CD

Installing Ubuntu from a Live CD is really easy. Just put the Live CD in the CD/DVD drive, close it, make sure your high speed Internet connections is connected (this will install needed updates from the Internet), and then reboot the computer. When the computer boots up from the Live CD, just follow the directions on the screen.

Once the installation is complete you will want to make sure that the daily updates from the Internet are turned on to retrieve new updates as they become available to keep your pc up to date with any and all updates. Attached are screen shot of Ubuntu to check your settings and make changes if needed. From the desktop panel bar, select the Systems icon, the Administration selection, and the Update Manager. See the cursor in the screen shot below:

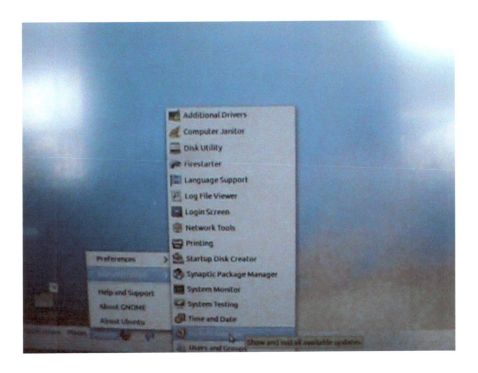

The next screen shot that will be displayed will be asking for your password in order to make any changes as seen below:

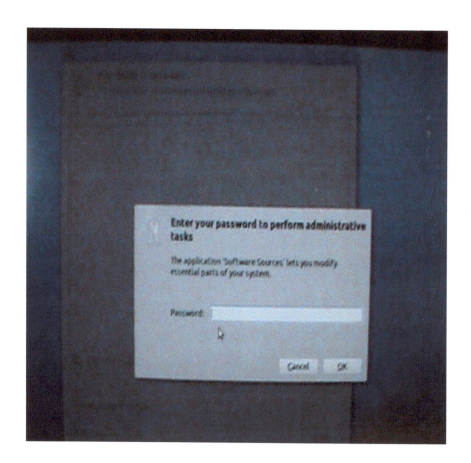

Type in your password and select OK to continue. The next screen you see will be the Your System is up-to-date screen. You will need to select the Settings selection at the bottom left of the up-to-date screen as seen of the screen shot below:

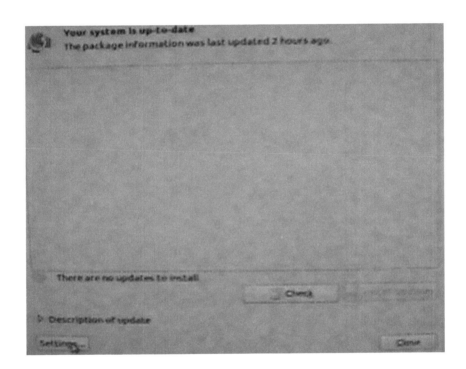

The next screen will be the Software Sources selection. Make sure all the boxes are checked as shown below and that the Download From: selection is the Servers for the United States (this selection can be changed but is best left to more experienced users).

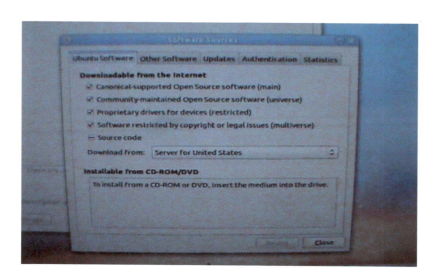

The next and last screen shot needed to check will be the Software Sources Update screen for the check for updates: Daily. If anything else is there, use the drop down arrow the right of this selection and change it to Daily (this is to get updates daily if any). Next check the selection of Show new distribution releases: for Normal releases. If anything else is there, use the drop down arrow to the right and change it to Normal releases. Then you can select the Close button at the bottom of this screen selection. If a screen pops up asking if you want to Revert or Close, select Close and it will save your changes.

See the screen shot below:

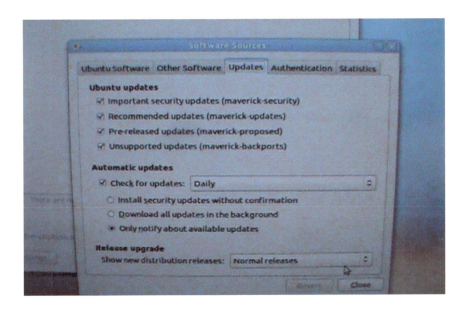

Screen shot of Ubuntu 11.04 Desktop

This screen shot is only on newer PC's. Older PC's will default back the old desktop. Here is a screen shot of the older desktop:

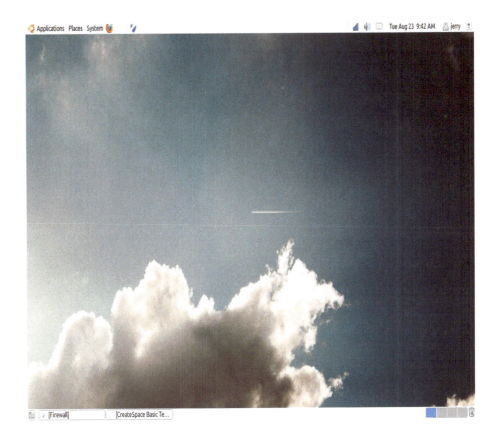

Broken PC Hardware

When turning on your pc the first thing to look for is if your computer can reach POST (power on self test)? Check the computer for blown capacitors on the motherboard. Most computers manufactured during the years 2000-2005 used defective capacitors on the motherboard. There is a world of information about this on the Internet. Major computer and motherboard manufactures have been sued over these defective capacitors. Here are some examples:

This capacitor is mushroomed.   This is a normal capacitor.

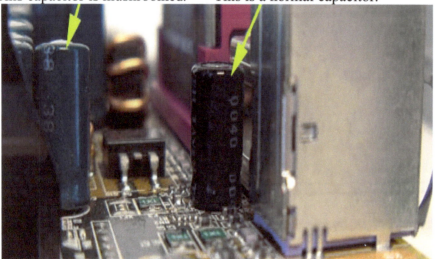

Capacitors tend to blow their tops and leak electrolyte, but as you can see from the pictures they can do a variety of things.

This capacitor has exploded and is leaking at the bottom.

This capacitor has exploded at the top and is leaking.

This capacitor has mushroomed, but has not opened up to leak any chemicals.

The capacitor below has lost its outer covering exposing the inside contents.

Discarded Computers

   People discard computers for many reasons. The replacement computers usually have Microsoft's operating system software. Not all of these older computers are physically bad. Some just need a good cleaning with a can of dust buster aerosol that can be purchased from most electronics stores and Wal-mart. Here is a picture of one of these products that come in many different brands and sizes.

How to Get One or More of Those Discarded Computers

One way to obtain computers that people want to get rid of is to advertise. Put in the advertisement that you will pick up the computer(s) that are no longer wanted. I have had people call to ask if I would buy their computer that is only a few years old. I have had to remind these people that I am not interested in buying computers. I am only looking for computers that are free and that I will come and pick them up.

I have fixed hundreds of computers this way and donated most of them to the Salvation Army since the markup on used computers are usually not worth the time to sell them. The Salvation Army sells them for a little money and what ever they get helps them to help the community.

However, you can occasionally find a decent enough computer to keep one for your own use as a spare. It is nice to have a spare computer or two when your main one breaks and needs a part. This way you can still have something to use until you can get your main computer fixed or replaced. I found a used computer driving by the scrap yard, while looking for something else, that was in pieces. The memory, CD rom, and the hard drive had been removed. After careful examination of the remaining parts I determined I would take it home, and see if I could make it work. To my surprise after adding the missing parts I turned the computer on and it worked. I installed Ubuntu Linux on it, and it is one of the fastest computers I have today, even though it was an old, used discarded Gateway pc.

Why People Hate Windows Operating Systems Software

Windows has such a monopoly on computer games for the market that most game developers do not want to write the code for other computer operating systems.

Microsoft OS will not let you uninstall Internet Explorer completely from your computer if you want to remove it for any reason. Microsoft doesn't play nice with the other operating systems. Windows is notorious for not providing support for networking with other operating systems on purpose.

All the default software that comes with Windows operating system is overstuffed with unnecessary things. One example of this would be Windows Media Player as opposed to Media player classic or VLC. You could spend around 30 minutes or more to remove unnecessary programs and services to speed up your computer.

At this time installing a new copy of Windows OS never seems to be able to activate itself over the Internet. More and more people have had to call Microsoft to get their window's software activated. Microsoft's automated telephone activation service never completes your new install, but Microsoft's people will activate the new install over the phone. They will do so without asking a single question about the software legitimacy that you have just installed. When this happens, this makes absolutely no sense to most people. A large number of users have learned that Windows OS software gets corrupted from time to time which requires a clean install to fix a number of problems. But users have to go through the authentication process to do this new install. A lot of people have resorted to making a ghost image of a clean install of XP to bypass this whole process headache.

How many times have you found that Windows cannot delete a file that is in use or sometimes cannot copy it? This headache is absolutely crazy. However, the Linux OS has been able to delete a file like this without a problem for many years. Have you ever tried copying over your own or someone else's, large Windows My Document file, started the copying process then walked away from the computer for a short period of time. Only to come back just to find an error message that it failed to complete the copy process? What a pain it is to find that it had stopped in the middle of the transfer process of all of the remaining files.

Have you ever found that the end task function process fails to do anything most of the time? How about when you try to end a task in Windows and then find yourself pressing the end task button selection a thousand times to try to end the task but end up just restarting the computer to fix the problem? There was a time that I only used Windows and I thought this was normal. I thought that sometimes things would just go into a computer twilight zone of no return and there was no way to end the program or the processes without restarting the pc.

The first time I was introduced to Linux was the early versions of Red Hat Linux and other types of Linux. I was amazed that a Linux version of end a task actually worked the first time that I used it and that it worked immediately. Auspiciously, I believe that this has more to do with the way the Kernel (core) of the operating system works. For Windows OS, I cannot find a fix for the end task function, that is an irritating problem. Have you noticed that every time a Windows OS Program(s) crashes such as the Windows XP OS that a pop up is displayed asking you if you want to send a useless report to Microsoft about this error? You would think if Microsoft was monitoring these reports that they could find a fix over time for the problem. They must get billion of these messages a year.

Reasons why Linux will prevail over Microsoft Windows

Unreliable Windows releases are the expected norm. One of the side effects you can always anticipate from Microsoft is to expect its new operating systems to be untrustworthy. Take a look at the history of its individual releases:
- Windows 95: Transformed personal computing from DOS (disk operating systems).
- Windows 98: An endeavor to improve on Windows 95 but it depressingly failed to make any improvements that are worth mentioning.

- Windows Me System was known as a practical joke by a large number of people.
- Windows NT Operating System made an effort to bring about an enterprise-level operating system to the computer world, except it required a near-genius in intellect person to get it working and keep it working.
- Windows XP System seemed like it had breathed new life back into the previously failing Windows operating systems that were a simple operating system. Windows Vista was even more disastrous than the previous failures.

Windows IS Annoying

I used an XP machine for work and I hated it. It was slow to boot even after Windows would show you a desktop. You still could not do anything for minutes, because it was doing security checks before releasing the computer for input. This is a design flaw in its software together with the need for anti-virus software. The software has a lot of other inadequately created background programs that just add to the problem.

The constant security updates are also annoying because they tie up your time to install them. Also you can not do anything until they are done installing and after the pc reboots. With the past history of Windows what else can we expect from Windows 7? I feel that any new Windows software will get a lot of hype but it is not worth the money it will cost to buy it or make other programs work with it.

I have a relative who bought a new computer with Windows 7 and tried to get into her Hotmail (now owned by Microsoft) email account. She found out that she could not use this email without purchasing yet another Microsoft add on program. She bought the program, installed it and still could not access her Hotmail account. She ended up canceling the cost of this add on software and stopped using this email account. Sound familiar to you? Microsoft sells you a new operating system then you have to buy yet another of Microsoft's add-on software programs to use it, when it should have just worked the first time. You have to ask yourself why people would put up with a company that keeps requiring you to spend money to use what you should have been using right along. It is beyond my comprehension that people would let things like this continue, but too many do.

Consistently, Linux has released its new software with reliable updates and fixes. Yes, there have been a few bumps along the way (Red Hat version 9 went from a free version to an enterprise system that costs money and Fedora 9). But for the most part, Linux has been steadily automating everything making it easier to install and load updates. Nearly all Linux distribution software has improved over the years to make it consistently more user friendly. Take a look at how desktops, end-user software, servers, security, administration tools, etc., have all become easier to use over time.

Windows has continuous price hikes. Microsoft has changed its licensing for Exchange to a per-user seat cost. Since changing this cost structure, anyone who logs on to an Exchange server must have a valid Microsoft license. So if a company has 100 employees (including administrators) who need to log on to Exchange server, it will end up costing the company more money. This creates a serious problem when a company starts having to spend more money for 500 plus Exchange licenses during our current times of shrinking budgets and less money to spend. This is not a good time for Microsoft to make such a daring change to licenses with the current state of the economy and companies holding spending to a minimum. Microsoft is creating a cost barrier while the world is facing serious recession. It is like Microsoft is pounding the nails into its own coffin and causing companies to reconsider other alternatives for their needs.

Linux operating software has Stable "prices". The prices of open source software licenses have remained the same $0.00 except for a few enterprise type Linux software systems, such as Red Hat Linux. eGroupware and Open-X-Change are outstanding groupware tools that have a larger set of features than Microsoft does. These two replacement software systems are reliable, scalable, secure, and free. The real cost you will have with these is the hardware that they are installed on. There is no limit to the number of users that can use this software, like Windows does with its per user seat license. One user or 1,000 users makes no difference with Open Source software.

Windows Incompatibility with Hardware

Microsoft Vista was a nightmare when it came to compatibility with different hardware. Vista was not only incompatible with a lot of the hardware; but it also required the newest computers with powerful processor and large memory to run the operating system. This was a windfall for the Intel Corporation to make a lot of revenue selling their newest processors. Intel recognized the potential of the public paying a higher price for newer processors because these had to be faster in order to run Vista. But even the newer processors were slow with Vista.

Linux has compatibility with most hardware, with a few exceptions like Lexmark printers. Lexmark built their hardware to run only on Windows software and refused to support most other operating systems. Linux software is making manual configuration of hardware a thing of the past.

Windows Makes Promises

Windows has been proclaiming that Windows 7 will be the best Microsoft operating system ever. However they have said this with every new release from Microsoft. Windows Vista was supposed to revolutionize the users' experience with the computer. Each Windows version was going to be better than the last and make it far simpler for the average user. Windows newer versions nearly removed every actual functioning part of the operating system to make it little more than a browser and an e-mail client system.

Microsoft has always been saying the next Windows release will redefine the personal computer to a better system. But the users have finally reached a point of apathy for Microsoft's new promises, so that they don't even care if something new is coming out.

The next release of any Linux distribution is never a mystery because the new release dates are always available to the public. Any user knows exactly when a release is due. All Linux distributions work under a full disclosure model with nothing to hide. For this reason, there is no false advertising going on with Linux. Unlike Microsoft, Linux never claims that its next release will revolutionize computing. Linux release dates are almost always on target.

Feature Comparisons

Microsoft proclaims that Windows 7 will run on any hardware that would run Vista and even hardware that is somewhat less powerful. What exactly does less powerful mean? One thing Windows 7 will have trouble with is the netbook market. The netbook market will run with Linux but Windows 7 requires more power than a netbook can provide. Netbooks can run on Linux Fedora 10 because the minimum system of requirements for Fedora resembles software of the 1990s.

Much of the computer world has already condemned Microsoft 7 to failure. Linux software is projected to surpass Microsoft in popularity by the computer world.

Reasons why Linux should be on your desktop

A few years ago, the Linux desktop was not as user friendly as it is now. Today Linux can out perform a wide range of tasks that are not even offered in any of the Windows versions of software for free.

Linux is gaining in popularity over Windows with each day that goes by. The Mac OS X Leopard has some interesting abilities but its cost is too expensive when compared to the cost of Linux. The visual perception of the Linux desktop is that it requires people to try something new, but it can provide plenty of delightful and interesting options.

With Linux, the first challenge is getting over the thought of trying something new and different. Some new computers can be purchased with some version of Linux installed. One of the good things about Linux is that installing Linux is no longer a challenge and it is automated. There are a handful of Linux distributions that are designed for simple and first time users. The benefits of Linux are many such as:

- The cost – Linux software is free with all of the applications. Microsoft is greedy and always has a high cost. The Vista Home Premium and Ultimate cost hundreds of dollars. Even if you upgrade from Windows XP it is going to cost you. Upgrading to any of the Office packages is not worth the price for what you get.

- Resources -- Even the most elaborate Linux distros require fewer resources than Windows XP to operate. The Vista operating system is a gluttonous single-user PC operating system that requires 2GB of RAM in order to operate at an acceptable speed, and at least 15GB of hard disk space.

- Performance -- Linux will work faster on a Dell Inspiron Core Duo than XP right out of the box.

- No bloatware -- Linux is free from adware, spyware, trialware, and unnecessary software to operate. Running Linux is like watching a fine watch keep time.

- Security -- Last year, 48,000 new viruses were created for Windows while Linux has had only 40 over the last ten years. Most Linux distros come with firewalls and anti-virus (AV) software that are free of cost.

Dual boot-able -- The best Linux distros make dual booting easy to do with the required hard disk partitioning without having to buy hard disk partitioning software.

Installation -- Anyone who has installed Windows knows it takes hours or even days before you get all the updates installed, and the applications up and running. Linux can take as little as half an hour to install the operating system, and utilities with a full set of applications. There is never a need for registration, activation, no paperwork, and no required phone calls like Microsoft requires.

Reinstalling the OS -- You are not allowed to just download an updated version of Windows. You are required to have the original CD that came with your PC and download all the Microsoft patches that have been made available since the CD was made. Linux is another story, you simply download the latest version of your updates (no questions asked) and they will install in the background. Your data files, previous settings, and favorites will stay intact. You don't even have to reboot from what you are doing. Linux can be shutdown when you and the up grade are finished for the day. Linux will install the entire down load updates the next time you boot your computer.

Keeping track of software -- With Windows, users have a shelf full of software CDs and have to keep track of all the serial numbers of installed software to be able to prove that it was purchased just in case you have to reinstall everything. With Linux software, there are no serial numbers or passwords to lose or worry about. Should you have to reinstall the software the passwords are then created by you during the installation.

Updating software -- Linux updates all the software on your system whenever updates are available from the Internet, including all applications programs. Linux places an update icon on your status bar to click on when new updates are available. Microsoft takes forever to download the updates. Then makes you wait until they are done installing to reboot the computer. After all that is complete, then you can do things on your pc. Linux doesn't ask you to reboot after downloading and installing updates. You can continue to work until you are finished for the day and then shut down your computer. Then next time you turn on the Linux computer, the computer is ready to go and you can do what you want without waiting for something to complete. XP will keep hounding you every ten minutes until you reboot your computer (what a pain).

More security -- These days, non-Microsoft operating systems are less vulnerable than the applications that run on them. It is for this reason that you need to keep your applications up-to-date with the latest security patches. Windows requires time consuming manual labor to do this, but with Linux everything is automated.

Defragging the hard drive -- Linux uses different file systems that does not require defragging. The Windows NTFS require constant defragging to try to keep the hard drive running as optimal as possible.

Operating system utilities -- The utilities inclusive with Windows are pretty much run of the mill. This is why so many 3rd party small software firms have made a nice living writing software programs to do it better for cost. Linux utilities programs are as good if not better than Windows freeware. Linux offers a number of free add on programs for CD burners to photo managers, memory monitors and disk utilities. Open Office Writer and the DTP application Scribus have a PDF conversion program already built-in. All you do is click a button on the task bar to save the file in PDF format. Windows would expect you to purchase a program to do the same task.

A few years back people were saying why Linux will not make it to your desktop because:
- The people who produce the product have no money for marketing.
- The reason they have no money is because they give the software product away.
- Since they give the product away, people rarely ever see Linux in computer software stores.
- Because people never see the product in stores or advertised, a large number of people don't know Linux exists or how good it is.
- The software programmers of Linux rely on word of mouth and the Internet to attract more users.
- On a closer investigation of Linux, you will discover that there are around 500 versions of Linux and growing. There is a version that is tailored toward anyone's special needs.
- After installing Linux and the user tries to use it, they would run into unexpected problems.

- When you asked the software developer manufacturer for help, they would suggest talking to other Linux users for help. These users would embrace your questions with enthusiasm but they did not always give you an answer to your questions that could be easily understood.
- When you explained to them that you are having trouble trying to understand them, you were often told that you need to learn the product to have a better appreciation of the software.

Some Linux software creators have said that they want to take to the world their software while other creators have said we should let the world come to Linux. Some of these software designers have said that their product is better than Windows and as good as anything that Apple has produced without the cost. Other designers just want to start work on the next newer version of Linux and not care what is going on in the world around them. It is hard to disagree with any of the Linux people when Linux is free to everyone.

Linux live CDs allow you to try Linux without installing it on your computer. How cool is that? You can try it, not install it, and it is free. Windows users will need time to adjust to the freedoms of Linux and that the cost is free. It is suggested that careful assistance is essential to avoid sudden shock when introducing Linux to Windows users that are not used to this type of computing freedom.

The Linux Economic Value Undertaking

In the last couple of years, some of the Linux software designers have designed the Linux desktops for the common PC users, and not just the computer savvy people. The main Linux OS that are user-friendly are LinuxMint, Linspire, Mandriva, Novell's SUSE Linux Enterprise Desktop (SLED to its friends), PCLinuxOS, SimplyMepis, Ubuntu (my favorite), Linspire and Xandros.

These distributions all include the operating system, a legion of user-friendly utilities and a full suite of Open Office, Internet web browsers, and Graphics with Multimedia applications. You can inspect all of these on the Live CD before you install Linux.

Installing Linux with all the current updates can take as little as half an hour with a high speed Internet connection. The installation process is mostly automatic and incorporates the setting up of the Internet connection. Common printers and scanners only need to be connected and turned on the first time during the installation process to be detected. They will be automatically installed but some could need some testing and selection of a generic setting before they will work.

These desktops present 3D graphics that surpass Vista and OS X in graphics display. Software updates are semi-automatic, and that includes all applications on the system. Linux never requires you to reboot your computer after completion. It will let you continue to do things and will complete the install the next time the computer is turned on. This software becomes appealing when Linux deemed that most of the desktop operating system costs next to nothing to obtain that includes all the applications that you might want.

If you're installing Linux on the same hard drive that has a Windows OS, you will need to create a new partition or two of unused space for the install. Linux Ubuntu offers to reduce the current Windows partition to a size that will allow Linux to be installed and also create the additional partitions that are needed automatically. Without the need of purchasing partitioning software.

Linux doesn't display C, D and E drives like Windows. Linux will display drives as sda1/dev or hda1/dev in the partitioning table. It is just a different way that drives are displayed and takes a little time to get use to.

Any Linux questions that you have, the answers can be found on the Internet at the most frequently asked questions website. If the answer is not found, you can ask the question by joining a help website called launch-pad and it is free of charge. Here are screen shots of the website:

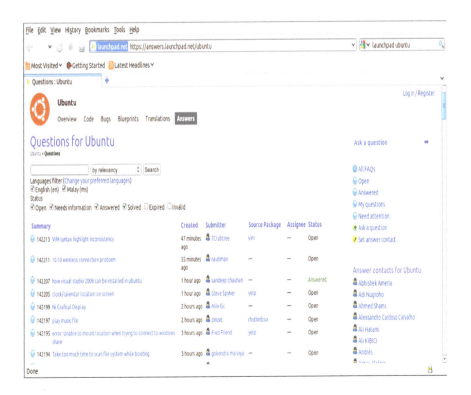

You will need to log onto the web site, registration is required to ask questions.

There your question(s) will be reviewed by people of the help community that usually have an answer posted within 24 hours. Some of my friends and I have used this help community to get answers to Linux problems encountered. SimplyMepis, LinuxMint and PCLinuxOS are the easiest Linux OS for newcomers to use and learn. I tested Live CD's for SimplyMepis, PCLinuxOS, Ubuntu and LinuxMint during August 2011. What's a live CD? It's an entire operating system, on a CD. The things you can accomplish with a live CD, from data recovery to virus removal to trying out cool operating systems.

Here is a screen shot of the LinuxMint-11-lxde desk top:

No Viruses!

When I think or hear of the main big name anti-virus software-for-profit programs for sale, I think of the **Maginot Line** of WWII history. The French created the Maginot Line as a fortification to allow time for their army to rally in the event of attack. This allowed the French forces to move into Belgium for a crucial confrontation with the invading German forces. With a defensive structure system in place, the French believed a successful direct attack from the Germans could be prevented. This thinking nonetheless was strategically unable to prevent the attack. The Germans invaded Belgium, and defeated the French army, by going around the Maginot Line at relatively unprotected areas (the weakest points of entry).

Hackers that write virus programs to infect anyone's computer are always looking for any weakness that they can use to exploit. No matter how well an anti-virus software is developed, there always seems to be a flaw that can be discovered.

I found that it virtually impossible to get a virus by disconnecting your hard drive and booting only to Live Linux CD. Only the memory is used with a Live CD to boot and access the Internet. This means that the PC is only using read only memory from the CD. Once the power is turned off, nothing is stored to anything that can be infected from a virus. The most a virus could possibly do is cause your PC to reboot since there is nothing that is connected to that get infected. If your DVD or CD drive is internal (inside your computer) must be set so it can boot from a Live Linux CD. There are three jumper pin settings on the rear of the drive. See the picture of drive.

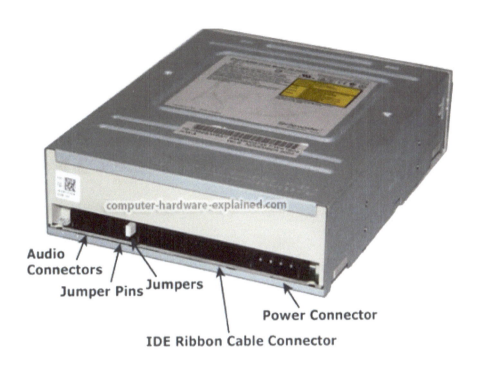

Audio Connectors

Jumper Pins **Jumpers**

Power Connector

IDE Ribbon Cable Connector

The jumper pin must be on one of the three settings that are label with a two letter code of CS, SL, or MS. A majority of computers boot this drive with the jumper pin on MS (master select) but other computers such as Dell computers use the jumper setting of CS (cable select) in order to boot from a DVD or CD Rom .

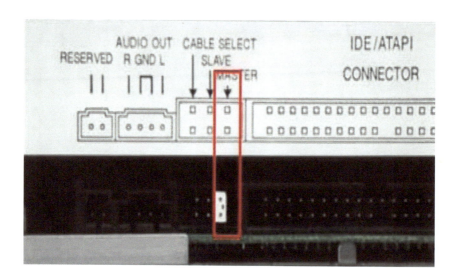

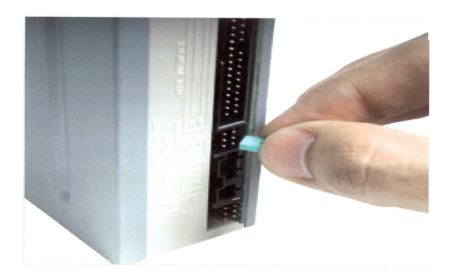

An external USB DVD/CD drive has no jumper pins to worry about. You want to use a DVD-R or CD-R when you burn the Linux image and not a DVD-RW or a CD-RW because DVD-RW or CD-RW are re-writable. The write once only DVD-R or CD-R prevent any chance of being appended. This prevents any chance of any virus from appending its self to a DVD-R or CD-R.

This means that anti-virus that costs money is not needed since there is nothing to infect (no hard drive connected). Imagine not needing big name anti-virus software like **Norton, McAfee, Trend Micro, Kasperksy** or **Symantec** to protect your computer while traveling the **Internet**! You can use free personal firewall software that is available for or already on some of the Linux Live CD's.

Computer Memory Needed

I have used a PC with as little as 500 megabyte of memory to run a Live CD to boot up the computer with no hard drive connected and connected to the Internet with high speed wired and wireless connections. I have tried three different Netgear USB wireless adapters. WPN111, WG111V2, and WG111V3 were tried on different types of computers with the different types of Linux Live CD's. Only the last two worked all different types successfully. Newer computers (last few years) can have between two to four gigabytes of memory on-board. It takes a couple minutes to boot up with a Linux Live CD with the hard drive disconnected. This is because DVD/CD drives run slower to load than a hard drive. If some needs to save a file like a word file, this can be easily done by just plugging in a flash drive to save it to and then eject it so nothing is connected for any length in time (this only necessary if the computer is connected the Internet). This is done only to limit any type of possible chance of a virus infection to a flash or USB drive (since it is removed, nothing is connected that can even possibly be infect should such a remote incident ever happen while on the Internet).

One draw back to using just a Live Linux CD is that a large number of people will not be willing to disconnect their hard drive to maximize their protection from a virus infection. These people will be their own worst enemy against a guaranteed way of protection.

Software Costs?

The Windows Office suite software is a high cost software add-on. Apple is expensive as well because you have to buy the Apple hardware at a premium price and then pay significant amounts of money to obtain any of Apple's software applications. The Linux Desktop by comparison with other OS is for the most part free, renders hardly any demands and operates on a Windows XP-spec computer without objections. Dell will sell computers shipped with Ubuntu Linux installed if requested by the customer. At the moment, which Linux version to install on a new computer is a marketing problem as to which version to promote!

Linux server administrators prefer lean, reliable, manageable Linux distributions, and it seems like Ubuntu has become the default Linux distribution. Ubuntu is not perfect for everything needed. Linux is all about having a choice. If you need and want something besides a standard system slowed down with all the bells and whistles, there are a lot of different types of Linux distributions to choose from to fit your needs. If you need a straightforward, lightweight, command-line based Linux for a server, an older desktop, a laptop, or if you just want to learn the Linux command-line better, they have many free choices to pick from at this web site **www.distrowatch.com.**

Linux evolves so fast that it is almost impossible for documentation in print media to catch up. Ubuntu Linux has millions of people that devote their time to innovating, fixing and produces a complete software revision every six months.

Camcorder and Camera

I bought a Sony Handycam from Walmart to take pictures and some cam-corded home movies. This camcorder came with a software drivers disc CD for Windows, but I use Ubuntu 10.10 instead of Windows. I hooked up the camcorder using the USB cord to my computer and Linux had their own auto recognition software drivers and programs that instantly recognized my hardware. I could immediately download videos and pictures to my computer without the hassles that Windows gives you with installing hardware drivers and licensed software to use my camcorder.

Things to consider about Windows

Microsoft had layoffs of 5,800 people company wide job cuts in 2009. Its stock has floundered the last ten years. This is a for-profit software company that pushed to market software that has not really been error-free or is overstuffed with unnecessary things that do not introduce anything new. The company forces you to pay for everything and prove that you have legal licensed software. They have always been saying the next Windows release will redefine the personal computer to a better system but fails to do so. Every day more people are realizing that this is a mature company that has reached a point where they come up with very few new products, and are falling behind at being an innovator in the computer world. Microsoft is trying to expand into other products like the X-box and their version of an Internet phone to expand their product lines. The company is in a downward trend of the computer for profit software market.

Things To Consider

My question to you is do you want computer software that is a downward trend of innovation or one that is (Linux) evolving so fast that it is almost impossible for documentation in print media to keep up (is old by the time books are printed). Ubuntu Linux has millions of people that devote their time to innovating, fixing and produces a complete software revision every six months. Windows cannot compete with this kind of innovation that is not-for-profit software. A large number of people are still unaware of Linux or afraid to try something new.